Caution in the Kitchen!

Germs, Allergies, and Other Health Concerns

Jennifer Boothroyd

Lerner Publications • Minneapolis

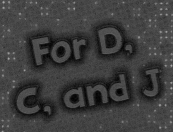

Lerner Publications Company
A division of Lerner Publishing Group, Inc.
241 First Avenue North
Minneapolis, MN 55401 USA

For reading levels and more information, look up this title at www.lernerbooks.com.

Library of Congress Cataloging-in-Publication Data

Boothroyd, Jennifer, 1972– author.
    Caution in the kitchen! : germs, allergies, and other health concerns / Jennifer Boothroyd.
        pages cm. — (Lightning bolt books. Healthy eating)
    Audience: Ages 5–8.
    Audience: K to grade 3.
    Includes bibliographical references and index.
    ISBN 978-1-4677-9473-2 (lb : alk. paper) — ISBN 978-1-4677-9669-9 (pb : alk. paper) —
ISBN 978-1-4677-9670-5 (eb pdf)
    1. Food handling—Safety measures—Juvenile literature. 2. Food handling—Juvenile literature.
3. Food contamination—Juvenile literature. 4. Food allergy—Juvenile literature. 5. Safety
education—Juvenile literature. I. Title.
TX537.B66 2016
363.19'2—dc23   2015016458

Manufactured in the United States of America
1 – BP – 12/31/15

Table of Contents

Eating Carefully

Food keeps us healthy. It gives us energy and nutrients.

Balanced meals help you stay healthy.

But sometimes, food can make us sick. Food can carry germs. Some germs can make your stomach very upset.

Tell an adult if you ever feel ill after eating.

Certain foods can also cause reactions in some people. An allergic reaction is when somebody gets sick from something that doesn't make most other people sick. Peanuts may be fine for you to eat. But they may give your best friend a rash. They may even make it hard for him to breathe.

It's important to make sure the food you eat is safe.

People can do many things to make sure their food is safe to eat. Let's find out about a few of them!

Making Food Safely

Washing your hands with soap and warm water is a good way to get rid of germs.

Always wash your hands before touching any food.

Rinse all fruits and vegetables in running water. It's a good idea to rinse even the ones you peel.

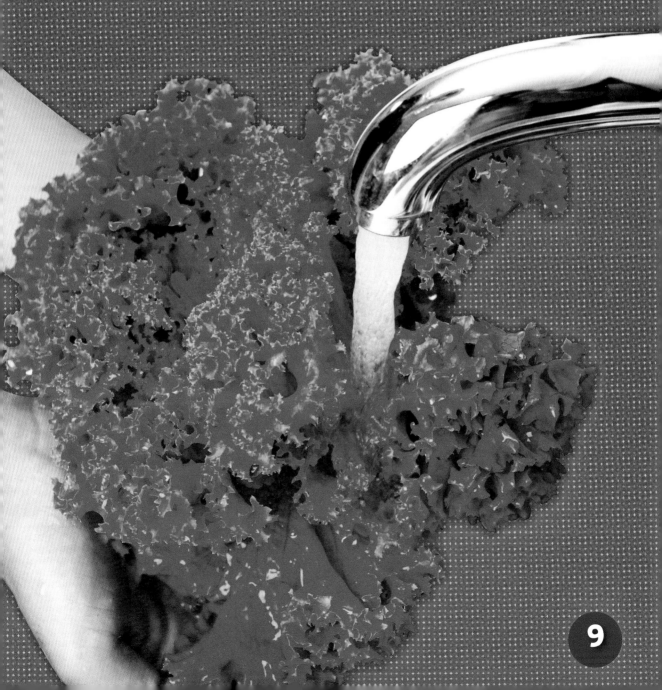

Be very careful with raw meat and raw eggs. The liquids from these foods can leave germs behind. And they splash easily. Be sure to clean off countertops after working with these foods.

Ask an adult to help you clean the counter after working with raw eggs.

You should also wash any dishes that touch raw meat or raw eggs.

Wash cutting boards between each use.

Frozen meat should be thawed in the refrigerator. It shouldn't be left out on a counter to thaw.

The fridge is the safest place to thaw meat.

Cooking food completely kills many harmful germs.

Storing Food Safely

It is important to store food carefully so it doesn't spoil.

Leftover pizza can make a good snack if you store it safely.

Airtight containers keep food fresh.

Containers like these can help keep germs out.

Many foods should be stored in the refrigerator.

Cold temperatures slow the growth of germs.

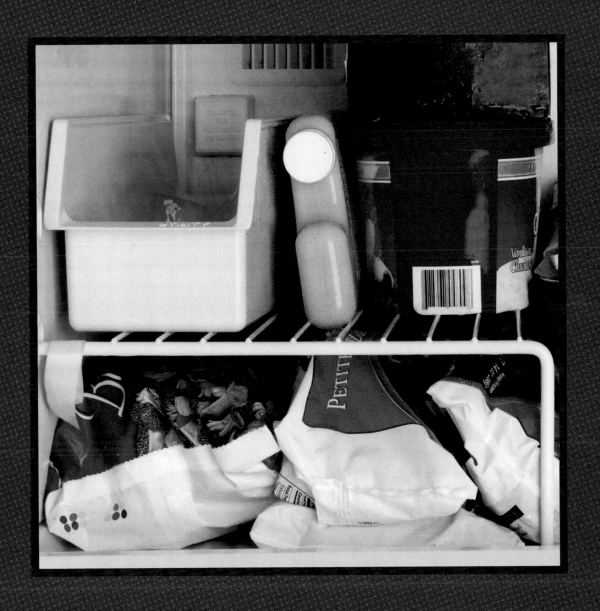

Frozen foods should be kept
in the freezer.

Some leftovers spoil very quickly. Store them in the refrigerator as soon as possible.

Pork and chicken dishes tend to spoil quickly.

Many foods have an expiration date. Foods shouldn't be eaten after this date.

Check for expiration dates on packages.

Choosing Safe Foods

People who have food allergies need to be extra careful about food. Other health conditions also call for extra caution.

Kids with food allergies need to be careful when eating at friends' homes.

These foods can cause stomach pain, itchy rashes, or even trouble breathing for some people.

Nuts, seafood, and eggs can cause allergic reactions in many people. People who are allergic to these foods must avoid them.

Other people may not have allergies, but some foods can still make them sick.

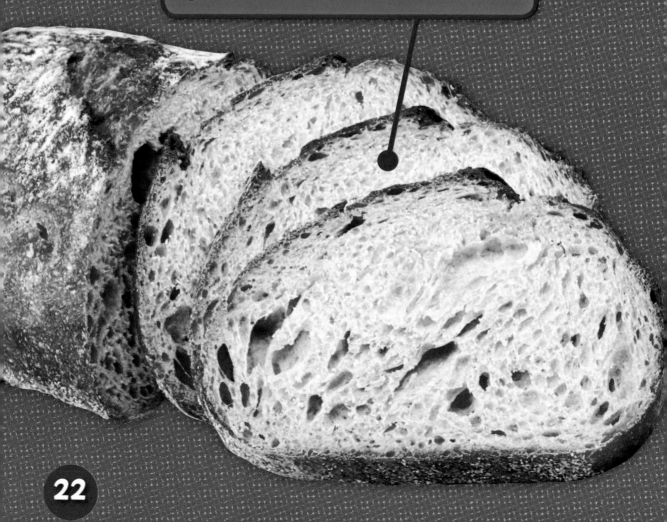

Some people are gluten intolerant. This means they can't eat a protein called gluten, which is in most bread.

These people have food sensitivities. Some foods hurt their insides. They must be careful when they order food at restaurants. And they must shop for foods that don't make them sick.

Many restaurants offer special food for people with food sensitivities.

Still other people have a disease called diabetes.

People with diabetes keep close track of the foods they eat.

People with diabetes need to make careful food choices. They need to keep their blood sugar regular.

This girl gets help checking her blood sugar levels.

Packaged foods have nutrition labels. People on special diets often check these labels. They list the ingredients and the nutrients in food.

Nutrition Facts

Serving Size 1 cup (240mL)
Servings Per Container about 8

Amount Per Serving

Calories 130 Calories from Fat 45

	% Daily Value*
Total Fat 5g	8%
Saturated Fat 3g	15%
Trans Fat 0g	
Cholesterol 20mg	7%
Sodium 120mg	5%
Potassium 360mg	10%
Total Carbohydrate 12g	4%
Dietary Fiber 0g	0%
Sugars 11g	
Protein 8g	

Vitamin A 10% • Vitamin C 0%

Calcium 30% • Iron 0%

Vitamin D 25%

You can check these labels too. Even if you aren't on a special diet, it's smart to look for healthy foods. Foods with lots of vitamins and minerals are good choices for everyone!

Oatmeal and other whole grain cereals often have lots of nutrients.

Try This!

Ask an adult if you can check the expiration dates of the items on a shelf in your fridge. If the adult says yes, look for dates on the containers on that shelf. If you see a date that is earlier than today's date, the item with that date has expired. Throw the item away. If you see a date that is coming soon, set that food near the front of the shelf as a reminder to eat it soon.

Fun Facts

- The temperature of your refrigerator should be at or below 40°F (4°C). An appliance thermometer can help you check the temperature.

- Rub your hands with soap for at least twenty seconds when washing your hands. That's about the time it takes to sing "Happy Birthday."

- Respect any special food needs your classmates may have. Don't bring peanuts near a classmate who is allergic to them. If you're inviting a classmate with a chocolate allergy to your birthday party, it's nice to provide him or her with a snack that does not include chocolate.

Glossary

allergy: a medical condition that causes a reaction to certain substances or foods

diabetes: a disease in which a person's body can't properly control the sugar in the blood

expiration date: a date by which a food may no longer be good to eat

germ: a tiny particle that can cause illnesses

nutrient: something needed by plants and animals to live and grow

raw: uncooked

spoil: to become too rotten to eat

thaw: to warm from freezing

Further Reading

Be a PAL to Friends with Food Allergies
http://www.foodallergy.org/document.doc?id=118

Bellisario, Gina. *Choose Good Food! My Eating Tips.* Minneapolis: Millbrook Press, 2014.

Fight Bac for Kids
http://fightbac.org/kids

Food Safety at Home, School, and When Eating Out
https://utextension.tennessee.edu/publications/Documents/PB1591.pdf

Food Safety Game
http://www.fsis.usda.gov/Oa/foodsafetymobile/mobilegame.swf

Index

Photo Acknowledgments

The images in this book are used with the permission of: © absolutimages/
Shutterstock.com. p. 2: © iStockphoto.com/monkeybusinessimages, p. 4: © Cavanagh
Ken/Science Source/Getty Images, p. 5: © Hong Vo/Shutterstock.com, p. 6:
© iStockphoto.com/subman, p. 7: © pixinoo/Shutterstock.com, p. 8: © Africa Studio/
Shutterstock.com, pp. 9, 15: © Simone van den Berg/Shutterstock.com, p. 10:
© iStockphoto.com/MidwestWilderness, p. 11: © Arterra Picture Library/Alamy, p. 12:
© Porsche Brosseau/Getty Images, p. 13: © iStockphoto.com/Allkindza, p. 14:
© iStockphoto.com/joebelanger, p. 16: © Nicholas Piccillo/Shutterstock.com, p. 17:
© littleny/Shutterstock.com, p. 18: © Sakarin Sawasdinaka/Shutterstock.com, p. 19:
© Eleonora Ghioldi/agency/Getty Images, p. 20: © iStockphoto.com/piotr_malczyk.
p. 21: © stocksolutions/Shutterstock.com, p. 22: © Ronnie Kaufman/Larry Hirshowitz/
Blend Images/Getty Images, p. 23: © ABK / BSIP / BSIP/SuperStock, p. 24: © Fertnig/
Getty Images, p. 25: © Martin Shields/Alamy, p. 26: © Josie Grant/Alamy, p. 27:
© Peter Dazeley/Getty Images. p. 28: © Anna Breitenberger/Shutterstock.com. p. 30.

Front cover: © Africa Studio/Shutterstock.com.

Main body text set in Johann Light 30/36.